D0775257

Tadeusz Różewicz

UNEASE

Tadeusz Różewicz

UNEASE

translated from the Polish by
Victor Contoski

woodcuts by Gaylord Schanilec

New Rivers Press 1980

Library of Congress Catalog Card Number: 79-57158
ISBN 0-89823-013-6

Book Design: C. W. Truesdale
Typesetting: John Minczeski

Some of these translations have appeared in the following publications: *Chelsea*, *Chicago Review*, *Chowder Review*, *Denver Quarterly*, *Fiddlehead*, *Grilled Flowers*, *Harrison Street Review*, *Midwest Quarterly*, *The Nation*, *New*, *Nightshade*, *Northeast*, *Stations*, *Stinktree*, *Sumac*, *Tuartara*, and the Quixote edition of *Four Contemporary Polish Poets*. Portions of the "Introduction" first appeared in *Books Abroad*.

We also wish to acknowledge, with gratitude, the grant assistance of the National Endowment for the Arts.

New Rivers Press Books are distributed by
SBD: Small Press Distribution
Jeanetta Jones Miller
1636 Ocean View Avenue
Kensington, California 94707

UNEASE HAS BEEN MANUFACTURED IN THE United States of America for New Rivers Press, Inc. (C. W. Truesdale, Editor/Publisher), 1602 Selby Avenue, St. Paul, Minnesota 55104 in a first edition of 1500 copies.

UNEASE

Tadeusz Różewicz was born in Radomsko in the district of Łodź in Poland in 1921. His childhood was marked by the economic depression of the 1930's, and he was forced to break off his formal education in 1938 because of financial difficulties. When Hitler invaded Poland, Różewicz joined the partisans; his teachers became the men he fought under — and against. After the war he settled in Cracow, where he studied art history at Jagellonian University.

His first volume of poetry was published in 1947. Since then he has written fourteen books of poetry, as well as several plays and short stories. (His plays have had successful productions both in Poland and abroad.) Translations of his poetry have appeared in Russian, Serbo-Croatian, Hungarian, German, Swedish, and English.

Currently he lives with his wife and two sons in Wrocław in western Poland.

In Tadeusz Różewicz we have at last a Polish poet who can be read without reference to the peculiar Polish historical context so necessary for an understanding of the Polish romantic poets, for while Różewicz treats Polish problems, he universalizes them in a manner readily comprehensible in the West. He writes primarily of the atrocities of the Second World War, and the crimes of Nazi Germany become in his work the primary symbol of our age.

His poems begin by concentrating on the everyday world. What might be called a "catalog of the ordinary" runs through his writing.

there is no color
no blue no yellow
no birds
no church steeples
no Mars no mound of Venus
no silver trumpets
("Head in Hand")

A room contains "a table three chairs/ a bookcase." ("Without Exaggeration") The people in his verse seem to perform ordinary actions. He describes a man walking as a man who "puts one leg down after the other." A man reads a book "on a Sundary afternoon/ in a little known town/ in central Europe." Sometimes his verse is so prosaic it seems flat.

The tables are set
with glass and porcelain
Every woman's hand
holding a rose
has five fingers.
("Warning")

Many a poet sees such natural phenomena as sufficiently poetic in themselves, but Różewicz goes one step further. He celebrates the natural, physical world, but only because it is a contrast to another world. His natural world is made poetic by its continual conflict, actual and implied, with the unnatural and unreasonable world that is continually and violently thrust upon it. A man is walking, but for Różewicz the fact that he "puts one leg down after the other" is poetic because the unreasonable world violently intrudes. The man is an epileptic who suddenly explodes into a savage, "foam like feathers/ decking his head." ("Epileptic") The peaceful man who reads a book is poetic not because he is reading a book, but because he is doing so at precisely the time when he should be making an important decision about two people who are awaiting sentence. The woman's hand with five fingers is contrasted by implication to an unnatural world in which women's hands have any number of fingers *but* five. (Later in the same poem the poet asks, "why do women have/ three black legs".)

Traditionally the poet has been able to turn from man and his follies and seek consolation in nature. In the curious world of Różewicz, however, man is denied even that. The rose and the moon are traditional poetic symbols, and it is interesting to examine Różewicz's treatment of them.

In "Magician" he compares the paper rose produced by a magician to the real rose of nature. His negative statements on the artificial flower may be taken as implied praise of the natural one when he writes that ". . . it lacks/ the bee's humming grain/ the silent grain of dew." Yet the natural rose is never physically present in the poem, and one is given not the adequacy of a natural rose, but the inadequacy of an artificial one.

In his short poem "The Moon Shines" the shining moon is secondary to the action of the poem. A man flees and is killed. The phrase, "the moon shines," is repeated twice at the end of the stanzas. The repetition here has at least a two-fold function: it contrasts the peace and quiet of nature with the degenerate world of man, and it emphasizes the moon as a terrible symbol of indifference — always an important emotion in Różewicz, since man is unalterable doomed. Though the poem is cryptically short, one might make out a case for the whole poem being a nature poem, i.e. the terrible action is not unnatural, but completely natural. Nature is as much a part of the violence as man.

This interpretation is supported by the role of nature in some of his other poems. In "Who's Missing" a good boy is drowned and changed into a monster. Whereas in "The Moon Shines" man is at least partially responsible for the violent action, here man is an innocent victim. In another poem the poet describes a burial. The dead man is put "in the earth/ like a child/ in its mother's lap." If the language seems a bit too sentimental, the last lines of the poem make the matter clear.

> they did not cut him off
> they did not throw him out
> he grows
>
> (untitled)

The mother, then, transforms her son into a monster. (One might advance the more traditional opinion that the body grows by turning into flowers, etc., but the poet has the corpse conscious through the action. There is no time given for decay and gradual transformation, since it begins growing as the mourners depart.)

Thus, if the poet takes refuge in nature, he is merely

deceiving himself.

How good, I can pick
berries in the woods
I thought
there are no woods
and there are no berries.
("How Good)

What remains for a man who is thus surrounded? In the poem "The Moon Shines" we have seen the moon as an important symbol of indifference. The man reading a book on a Sunday afternoon is able to do so because he is indifferent to the tragedy he might be able to prevent. In the poem "I See the Mad" the poet is able to sail the ocean only because he knocks off his boat the hands of those drowning people who believed they could walk on water. The prodigal son returns home thinking those he left will be happy to see him, but he is greeted with indifference and concludes his only recourse is to be indifferent also.

nobody knows I have returned
there is still time
I shall go
nobody will know
I was here and was not
("Prodigal Son")

Again, a seeming indifference is the only solution of the Jester (surely a figure of the poet). Only the Old King understands him, but he cannot bear to be understood. He laughs the King to scorn.

Nevertheless a sensitive man because of his very nature cannot be indifferent. Hence a strong tone of irony in Różewicz's work, and hence the dramatic conflict that makes his poetry so exciting. The conflict between reasonable and unreasonable worlds parallels the conflict between love and indifference. In a poem entitled "To the Heart" the poet describes a cold-blooded specialist tearing the heart out of a living sheep. The editorial comment is brief: "yes sir/ that was/ a specialist." But the poet is not as indifferent as he pretends. The title has two meanings. The specialist extends his hand through the sheep's throat "to the heart," but the poem is also addressed to the heart of the poet and the reader, that the heart may learn how necessary indifference is in a world of such specialists. Even when the poet knocks the hands of drowning men off his boat, he notes that they are human; he is "cruelly alive." With one adverb the poet lets us know he is not like the specialist. People are people, and not sheep. When the Jester laughs at the Old King, it is not a gesture of indifference after all. The Jester is bitter, savage, and desperate. His action is not the action of a man who does not care, but of a man who cares too much.

Thus the "natural" world of Różewicz is not natural at all in the traditional sense of the word. His world contains both natural and unnatural phenomena as organic elements, mixed in such a relationship that the terms themselves are almost meaningless in his verse. The only way a man can exist in such a world is through indifference. But the impossibility of a sensitive person attaining this indifference gives dramatic value and immediacy to much of his poetry.

In translating these poems I have tried to maintain the literal sense of the Polish text, while attempting likewise to retain some sense of the flow of the poetry. Inevitably, however, some of the sharpness of the original is lost. In my version of "To the Heart," for example, I use almost twice as many words as in the original. And instead of translating fragments of nursery rimes and children's songs literally, I have sought equivalent poetry in English. I hope these translations nevertheless convey some of the exciting visions and dramatic techniques of one of the fine poets of our time.

I wish to thank my wife, Wiesława, for her help in checking the accuracy of the translations, and the General Research Fund at the University of Kansas for its support of this project.

I

from *CZERWONA REKAWICZKA*

(1948)

I SEE THE MAD

I see the mad
who walked on the sea
believing to the end
and they went down

even now they tilt
my uncertain boat

cruelly alive
I knock off their stiff hands

knock them off
year in year out.

THE MOON SHINES

The moon shines
the street is empty
the moon shines
and a man flees

the moon shines
the man fell
the man died
and the moon shines

the moon shines
the street is empty
the face of the dead
is a puddle of water.

THE TREE OF REGRET

All day long
grows the tree of regret
the tree of rain
fog words and silence

the express
cracked into
the steel rib of a bridge

In the recess the engineer
left for the poor
I await my departure

My regret rises and falls
one tear dissolved
this world of iron
cement and gold

It's you are the crown
of the tree which grows
in me from morning
to night.

AT MY FEET

A little blue ball
from childhood
rolls away from my feet
and further on

uncatchable
I run after it in vain
greedy hands outstretched

it flows silently
from the eye of a mother
bending over

it rolls like laughter
pearl after pearl

a juggler
has lured it to his hand

oh how lightly
and carelessly
a stranger
entertains people
with my happiness.

HOW NICE

How nice. I can pick
berries in the woods
I thought
there are no woods and berries.

How nice. I can lie
in the shade of a tree
I thought
now trees don't give shade.

How nice. I am with you
and my heart pounding
I thought
man has no heart.

II

from *SREBRNY KŁOS*

(1955)

WITHOUT EXAGGERATION

I tell a story
of limited interest

the burning of poems
takes place in silence
it is a rite empty
of pathetic gestures

the burning of poems
takes place among
usual decorations
a table three chairs
and a bookcase

the paper burns
the flame dances
smoke rises

When the words were born
he shouted
who now is silent

fire devours him
and the ashes mingle

IT TRIES

Sometimes poetry
reminds one
of the hands of an infant
wanting to grasp everything

The hand submerged
in the universe
tries to close
into a fist

Tries to enclose
the fruit
the perfect form
but is weak
open
and the fruit falls
heavier and heavier
greater and greater

WHO'S MISSING

Who drowned
who's missing

Who screamed so
who's silent

who has no mouth

What is it
that rises
the small body
terribly grown

such commotion so many words
who's missing
it's he
that good boy
he changed
into a thing
which comes silently
from the water
and butchers its mother

PARROT

In my home town which the mayor in his derby
could walk through in half a day
in the town where
for many years
it was said
that old lady Szlojmina had a child
with the head of a carp
and knife-grinders rag-pickers
musicians gypsies
jugglers
and Chinamen selling silk
hiding their rainbows
in locked suitcases
walked through the alleys

Sometimes
an organ-grinder came

A fantastically-colored parrot
emerald feathers glowing
slowly pulled out a paper
with our fortune on it
as music triumphant music
filled heaven and earth
grew hoarse
and died out
in the wooden box

And we with flushed cheeks
discovered our fate
a fake glass ring

The organ-grinder
packed up music and parrot

but its strangely curved beak
and talons
remained
long drowned
in our dreams

PRODIGAL SON

(from a painting by Hieronymus Bosch)

Between the closing
and opening of a door
in the inn
"Under the White Swan"
between the opening
and closing of a door
what happened
so many springs
winters autumns
fled

between the closing
and opening of a door
I saw life
with a wolf's jaw
a pig's snout
under the hood
of a monk
the open guts of the world
I saw war
on earth and in heaven
crucified people
who redeemed nothing
scepter and globe
rotting in the palm

I saw the world's end
and its beginning
between the closing
and opening of a door
in the inn
"Under the White Swan"

I saw earth
through a rain
of tears and blood
shining
with corpse light

beer I drank
"Under the White Swan"
here the beer is flat
nothing but dishwater
tossed down my last
battered penny
long the waitress
looked it over
thinking it counterfeit
and my face also
carefully studied
I went out
nobody knew me
none looked into
my torn countenance
the man in the corner
with his back turned
that's my friend

I bring no presents
in this big basket
cat skin
brought me no luck
no one greets me
no one knows me
the world is complete
without me

at my going Maggie
white as an open fruit
closed the door
by a hag the door

was opened by a hag
hideous and flaccid

nobody knows I have returned
there is still time
I shall run away
nobody will know
I was here and was not

the caged bird
over the door
sings like a record
there in the world
I wept away the nights
I thought every house
would extend a glad hand
every branch bird and stone
come to my reception

I shall not go
into that house
everything is old here
dirty and small
older and more filthy
and less than I am
and I thought
I return to the nest
the star
my brightest star
in wandering
through night
ashes
fire of the world

run for it
disappear before
I'm recognized
by that old hag
looking out the window

"Under the White Swan"

I thought my place
awaited me
now I see
I had no place
I thought a vacancy
remained when I left
but life
like water
filled it already
I am like a stone
pressed in the depths
rock bottom
I am as though
I were not

those
the provident
who remained where they were
worked hard
for themselves
they think
they are irreplaceable
at that table
that the rising sun
inquires about them

I went out
and they remained
here in the inn
"Under the White Swan"
they disappear from my sight
and they see me not
I go faster now
farther and farther

never to return

MOMENT

Poplars like grapes
on the old silver
of the cloudy sky

maybe here I'll find
what I really need

here's a girl
who went by
and with the most beautiful gesture
at this moment
on earth or in heaven
pushed back her hair
flowing with light
on her proud shoulders

mountains smoke
in the ash of heaven

I'll stay here
that's right
I don't need anything

Shadows on the walls
of small silent houses
and a bright shadow
on the balcony

the heart beats again
that died in that place
strange as a star
Verona

STONE BROTHERS

"Liegen und Ruhen
in einer Gruft
Unter diesem Stein"
say the Gothic letters
sharp as swords

In the Cathedral of St. James
in Nysa

Two marble brothers
small boys
Johannes and Fredrich
died in April and May
three centuries ago

they stand motionless
in a marble recess
and hold cold hands

the noise was terrible
when the city fell
at midnight the sirens howled
it was bright
and red
as if all blood
were drawn off
onto the empty streets

Bells fell
from the cracked belfry
by the Cathedral of St. James
their tongues struck the earth
children smothered in basements

the old square
glowed like coal
smoke bitterly
went out

Johannes was ten years old
and Fredrich   four
they died in April and May
say the Gothic letters
sharp as swords
the small brothers watch
how roundabout
the great world
changes

III
from *UŚMIECHY*
(1957)

MAGICIAN

From the sleeve or ear
of one of the audience
appears in his hand
a paper rose

"Almost like real . . ."
(or more than real
more spectacular)

Only that it lacks
the bee's humming grain
the silent grain of dew

Only that dust settles
year after year
on the dead petals

SINS

The priest sat in the confessional
with a great face of white cheese
a purple stole on his neck
I crossed myself and began
"Bless me father for I have sinned . . .
my last confession was
since then I have offended God
by the following sins:

I ate meat on Friday
out of gluttony
uh. . . .
I didn't want to get up in the morning
to go to school because I was lazy
I wrote a dirty word
on a fence
um. . . .
I looked at a picture
in daddy's big book
ah. . . .
during mass I thought about
the white mice
daddy was supposed to give me
for my birthday
I didn't say my prayers
two times
I ate a bag of candy
and got sick
I called my playmate names
but he stuck his tongue out at me

For all these sins I am heartily sorry
and promise to amend my life"

I heard a knock
on the oak confessional
beat my breast
kissed the rough gold
cross on the purple stole
went out
and my sins were forgiven

NOTES FROM A MUSEUM

I

"Madness"

"Madness"
the blind stallion of desire
falls into the abyss
with a woman's alabaster body
Gold and tar
smoke and fire
ruby

two soldiers
wink at each other
and the guide explains:
"it is
realistic symbolism
under capitalistic conditions"

the black horse neighs
and we go on

2

There are museums in which
the chair on which Shakespeare
did not sit
stands before the table
on which Moliere did not work

Here is the slipper
of Madame de Pompadour
like a silver shell

carelessly tossed off
the owner
is not yet awake

Caesar's high hat
his snuff box glasses
and pants
whose authenticity
and hoary age
the silent moths attest

rest in eternal peace

3

Frame

"Nice work grandma
sitting among beautiful pictures"

The old woman shrugs her shoulders

"What's nice about it?
There's never enough heat
and I have to sit here all day

it's so cold
a person just turns blue"

IV

from *FORMY*

(1958)

FORMS

Those forms once so well set
obedient always open to the reception
of dead poetic material
terrified by fire and the smell of blood
broke and dispersed

they turn on their creator
rend him asunder and drag
him down interminable streets
where long since
marched all orchestras
schools and processions

still-pulsing meat
brim full of blood
feeds
these perfect forms

so tightly converging over the spoils
not even silence
escapes

KING

In loneliness
when they set his bowl of food
before him
he mutters trembles
licks his chops

a bag of bones

thou art the lord of creation
— I say to him —
when you look
the lion squints
thou art lord of the world

thou art Socrates Caesar
Columbus Shakespeare
hast formed sonnets
split atoms
built gas chambers
raised the cathedral of Notre Dame

thou hast opened the maws
of stone chimeras
and it is nothing that now
they laugh
at you and at me

with a bone in his teeth
he flees
and I after him crying

thou art lord of creation
king
and cathedral

JOB 1957

Earth heaven the body of Job — dung
heaven dung
eyes dung
lips

what remained
was begun in love
what grew has ripened
what was merry
is changed to dung

earth heaven the body of Job
rose dung
lips dung
heaven

what was wrapped in caresses
what was clothed in dignity
what rose up
has fallen

through sky through sun
through silence through lips
come the flies

DOOR

The masons went away
and left a perpendicular hole in the wall
Sometimes I think
my place is too conventional
anybody can get in

If the masons had not left
that hole in the wall
I would be a hermit

tough

I spend my time
coming and going
lately I put in revolving doors
through which
enter the affairs of the world

an apple tree in bloom
never stood there
nor a small pony
with a wet eye
nor a star nor a golden bee hive
nor a stream with fish
and buttercups

but I will not wall up the doorway
maybe a good man will stand in it
and tell me who I am

IN HASTE

He was reading a book
on a Sunday afternoon
in a little known town
in central Europe

in the other hemisphere
dark now
two people
awaited sentence

far off a train rumbled
daylight in the room
it could have been one o'clock
he felt
he must decide
action must be taken
at once
after all twenty years he waited
knew that he had to choose
that it was the last moment
wanted to do something

but couldn't remember
what it was
forgot
deeper and deeper

alongside him others moved lively
were born and died in haste

I AM A REALIST

Now everybody waits for the mailman

My younger son holds a ladybug
and sings, "ladybug ladybug fly away home"
the seven year old
stands confused by the table
and says
"but there are too angels daddy"
mother makes coffee
says
"how my hair is falling
I want to buy a blanket for father
this one's like a sieve
every morning the old man gets up
covered with feathers"

I take an apple from the table
and go to work
where I will write concrete poems
for twenty years I am working
on one poem

I am a realist and a materialist
only sometimes I'm tired
I close my eyes

V

from *ZIELONA RÓŻA*

(1961)

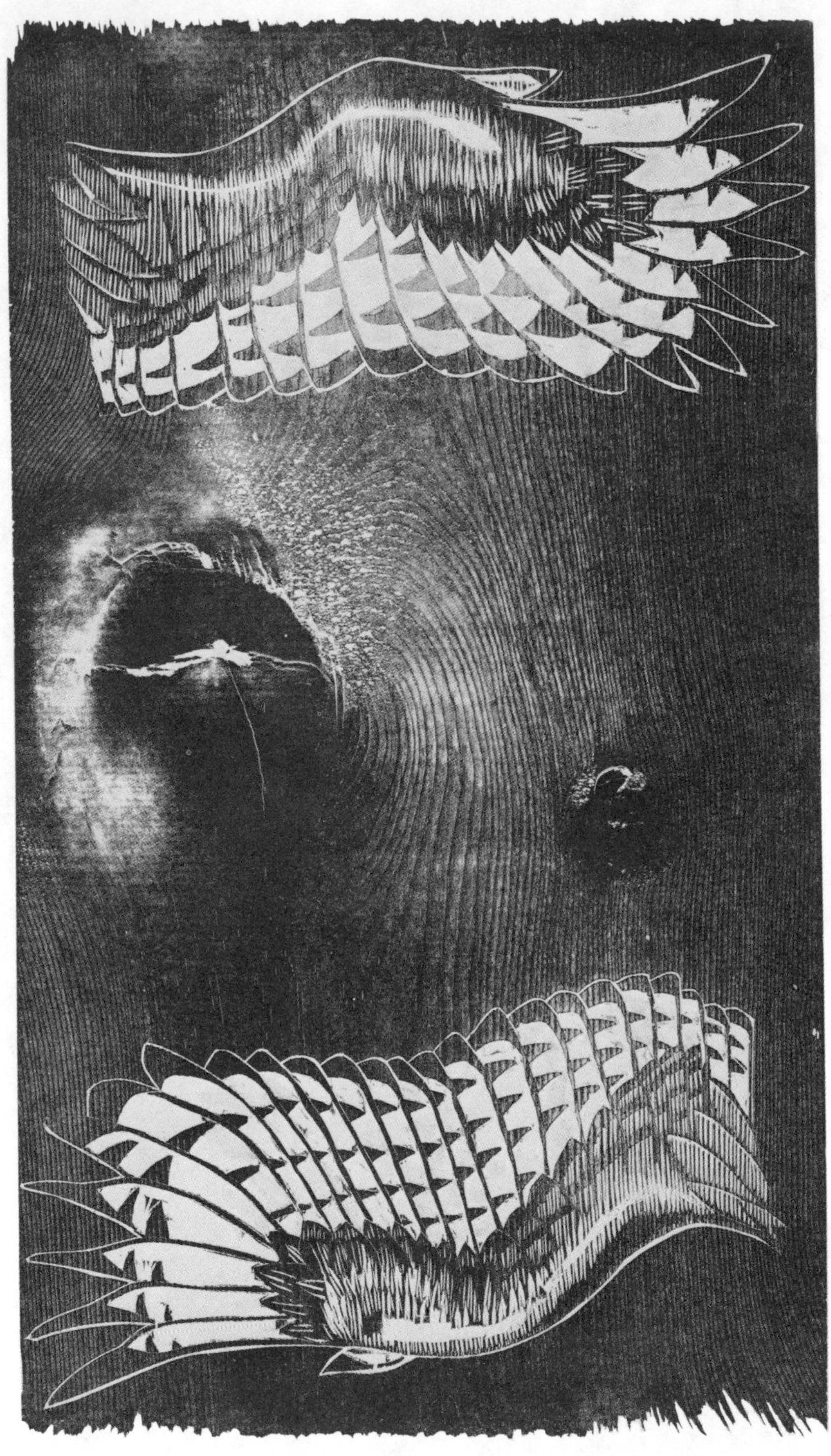

FIGHT WITH AN ANGEL

The shadow of wings grew
an angel crowed he hummed
his wet nostrils
touched my eyes my lips
we fought on earth
made of trampled newspapers
on a garbage dump where
blood spit and bile
lay mixed with
the dung of words

the shadow of wings grew
and lo
there were two wings
huge from ear to ear
rose-colored
among the clouds
on both sides of the head
our excrement covered
the playing field
and at last
he overpowered me
bound me dazzled me
with the word
drooled
chatted optimistically
and ascended the heaven of poetry

I grabbed his legs
and he fell
by the wall
into my garbage

and here am I
the form of a man
with light in my eyes
like thumbs

ROOTS

Photosensitive
aesthetes
with one eye
speaking of Van Gogh
paint suns
brush the banal branch
of the blossoming almond

I see him at night

I see him
in Borinage
underground
fire
devours people
with eyes
with beating heart
with tongue
surging through
the walled shaft

heaven is high
and rises higher
the eyeless mole
Van Gogh
touches light

looking at sunflowers
I think of roots
buried in the earth
pushing toward the sun
not knowing
light
crown

when a stranger greeted me
in the middle of the night

I knew him

DANTE'S GRAVE IN RAVENNA

Dante
There's nothing here
Look it's empty
Tourists sunglasses
red eyes blue lips
orange hair
heads soft-boiled
thinking of beauty
Let's go on
Wait your turn
There's nothing there
They look through the keyhole
Dantis poetae sepulcrum
The one-legged man
who sits in the corner
ashamed says
That's all
there's nothing more
Steel chains
Brass wreath
Virtuti et Honori
Padlocked
in the chapel
Dante
it's empty
there's nothing
there

TO THE HEART

I saw
a specialist a cook
place his hand in the mouth
push it down
through the sheep's throat
touch the beating heart
close his fist on it
and tear it out with
one jerk
yes sir
that was
a specialist

# # #

They threw earth on the coffin
on the open eyes
on the light

he saw them
from the side
retreating
deeper

he remained
in the language of his country
in the earth
like a child
in its mother's womb

they did not cut him off
they did not throw him out
he grows

JESTER

The jester
was too clever
to laugh
at others

too clever
or too sad

so they laughed at him

his only equal
was the Old King
only the Old King
understood him
so he laughed the King
to scorn

RELIEVING THE BURDEN

He came to you
and said

you are not responsible
for the world or its end
that burden was taken from your shoulders
you are like birds and children
have a good time

and they do have a good time

they forget
that contemporary poetry
is a fight for breath

IN AN OLD SHRINE

In a shrine
of eight hundred Buddhas

one yawns
the second has long eyebrows
the wings of swallows
the fifth is angry
the third scratched in the heel
the sixth listens to the song
of a bird sitting
on a gilt hand

the tenth raises a sword
the ninth a lotus flower
a smoky moon

trumpets
wafts of incense
gongs

the monks are silent
bead by bead
they count their prayers
with dirty fingers

a yellow skull
of polished bone
eyes
lowered

maybe he thinks of the meat
he has given up
of the tongue of a woman
maybe of a bird
that he held in his hand
ages ago

how its heart beat

HOUSE

I am the house of the dead
they found here
their last shelter

motion of hands
in my direction
take me
with you take
don't let go

I was opened
and they began living
in cold
empty
dark

such is
their world without end
such the forgiveness of sins
resurrection of the body

and life everlasting

THE FAMILY OF MAN

There was no star
over the barn no wise men
or angels

A woman bites a shawl
between her teeth
so that no one will hear her cry

The carpenter is silent
he looks on in darkness
he did not believe in a miracle
the night grows
so does the cross

And people
hung up a star
because it was too dark for them
it was empty
a chill was emanating
from that mystery
And they sang

Hark the herald angels sing,
Glory to the new-born king,
Slee--eep in heavenly pee-eeace

Something from the heaven's heights
Dropped down into my insides,
Slee-eep in heavenly peace.

ANONYMOUS VOICE

So long I shaped
myself
to the form and image
of nothing
I shaped the face
to the form and image
of everything

at last the features are blurred
my words
fit

I WROTE

I wrote
a moment or an hour
evening night
I was seized with wrath
I trembled or dumb
I sat beside myself
my eyes filled with tears
I was writing a long time
suddenly I discovered
there was no pen in my hand

AT THE SAME TIME

Ten thousand miles
I flew from home
they dressed me fed me
like a baby

ten thousand miles
I flew from home
flew in the stars
a humming lyre
air between the strings

so far flew the void
angry and agitated

nothing filled it no dragons
lions golden eagles octopuses
pagodas
heavenly temple
or pearl
when an empty man flies so far
a corpse flies among stars
and nothing wakes him
neither names of foreign cities
nor cold sirens of dawn
untouched by tongues of fire
which stand over the fields
he sleeps with a polite
smile on his lips
bows and
speaks

he wakes neither to a small bell
or transparent porcelain

nor to the rumble of mountains
being moved

nor to the names of flowers

dragon's jaw
tiger's paw
yellow crane
a shade on the window
red lips
nor a dream of flowers

hoarse voices
a gurgle in darkness
in felt soles
they carry great burdens
run lightly quickly a bird
I with this small burden
with one thought only
heavily and unwillingly go
down to the depths of a dream

in the imperial summer residence
I-Ho-Yen
a lotus leaf on the water
the form of
the empire passed
the emperor a dragon
the empress a peacock
golden fish swim
fish veils
the sundial stops night

one thousand poems
written in the railroad factory
on old newspapers
in black India ink

perfect poetry
was painted
glued to the walls
hung on construction sites
over the machines
it moves lightly
in silken shawls
in colored sashes

under a cloud a flock of black birds
what kind of birds
in the window branches of a tree
what kind of tree
on the floor
at the foot of the bed
woven blue dragons
battle without respite
when I close my eyes
and open

the old face of a farmer

his old face
is prepared
to welcome my smile
there is a smile in it
hidden
plowed under in the depths
it waits
one must invoke
the smile hidden
in that wrinkle
in the furrows of the face
which is earth already

sunlight
fills the valley

the sundial in the summer residence
stops
night I-Ho-Yen
golden fish swim
fish veils

I drink tart green tea
with a white flower
of jasmin

at the same time

a vase like a drop of blood
rises
pirouettes
shines waxes full
sets
goes out
on a girl's finger
in a Chinese circus

at the same time

motors roar in yellow dust

at the same time
horses and oxen pull trucks

at the same time
men and women
in blue overalls
pull wagons
in the biting dust

at the same time
on a huge yellow river
high on a wave
the sail of a lonely boat

our ship goes off
and I will never say anything
to those people

the boat sails
and two people
a man and a woman
disappear

at thc same time

we go
with small white masks on our lips
smiles
two little blind elephants
among china

VI

from *NIEPOKÓJ*

(1964)

HEAD RESTING ON HAND

He sees no color

All people
have one eye
one head with no face
set on a crate

all tastes
have one taste
all smells
one smell
all sounds
turn into
a protracted moan

there is no color
no blue no yellow
no birds
no church steeples
no mars no mound of venus
no silver trumpets

the head he sets
in the hand
is a heavy head
resting on the hand
of another person

there is no history

the one
who sits on the bench
says

it is his head
resting on my hand

he repeats one word

once he thought
he lacked words
but it turned out
one was sufficient
one sound
not too clear

THE MOTHER OF THE HANGED

She brushes against the rough skin of the crowd.

Here
on the street she walks
the mother of the hanged
a black woman
carries a silver head
in her hands
oh what a heavy lump
filled full of the night
bursting with brilliance

confused she wanders
in shoes with crooked heels
singing singing
with her empty womb
with her withered breasts
the confused siren howls
to the swollen moon over the city

with leaden steps
she walks the pavement
the mother of the hanged
the moon at her throat
she goes under
brushing against the rough scales of the crowd.

LITTLE AMBER BIRD

Autumn
a transparent
amber bird
from branch to branch
carries a drop of gold.

Autumn
a luminous ruby bird
from branch to branch
carries a drop of blood.

Autumn
an azure bird
dies
from branch to branch
falls a drop of rain.

WINGS AND HANDS

When I go onward
do not hold me back
that is the road into light

hands from all sides
busy hands
scatter and diffuse me

and the tracking starts
and the interplay
of light and hands begins
And there are shadows

On the white clouds
the shadows of hands and wings
though there are no angels among us.

I SCREAMED IN THE NIGHT

I screamed in the night

the dead stood
before my eyes
silently grinning

cold and dead
a blade from the darkness
went into my body

opened
my guts

WOOD

A wooden Christ
from a mystery
of the Middle Ages
goes on all fours

in crimson splinters

in a collar of thorns
with the hanging head
of a whipped dog

how the wood
thirsts

GOLDEN MOUNTAINS

The first time
I saw mountains
I was twenty-six
years old

I did not laugh
or shout
in their presence
I spoke in a whisper

When I returned home
I wanted to tell
my mother
how mountains look

It was hard to say
at night
everything looked different
mountains and words

Mother was silent
tired
maybe she slept

In the clouds
the moon grew
the golden mountain
of the poor

LEAVE US

Forget us
our generation
live like people
forget us

we were jealous
of plants and stones
jealous
of dogs

I want to be a rat
I told her then

I don't want to be
she said with eyes closed
I want to sleep
and wake up after the war

forget us
don't ask about our youth
leave us alone

UNCLEAR VERSE

In Memory of Leopold Staff

1

It was only a thousand
threads they bound him
with a thousand
weak threads

to this world
this beheaded world

they bound him with one hair
to silliness and poetics

They bound me
to old landscapes
forefathers' bones
and superstitions

they bound to
they bound with one hair

look to what
they bound me
by one hair
to a falsifier of words
another hair
to a cathedral

he pretended he didn't feel
the weak threads
he could break each
hair individually each
black and white thread

he went out gently
not breaking the threads
he left
all the bonds intact

went out dragging behind him
a net

2

Comes the great light
cruel and cold
cuts him off swallows Him
spits him out And dies

he who invoked it
who waited
is afraid

How he clings
with all hands
how he smiles humbly
and closes his eyes
not to see the light
which comes
and cuts the bonds

So I must be alone
and where are the nice little things
warm corners
seeds and trifles
which bind one to life
where is a blade of grass
give me one blade of grass

I lived in black slime
but there were people in it

animals and plants
landscapes and stars

there was a house
with windows you could open
and stairs you could walk up

3

He left his work
the weaving
of the world's darkness
harmony and light

the sword is silk
the sword which falls
the sword which hangs
over our heads

he waited patiently
bound to a woman
to wine to tall trees
to a small dog

what cruel brilliance
he had to force from himself
to cut the frail threads
tied by weak beings

4

I wove from my essence
mourning and covered
trees birds and water

everything drowns
in my dreary sadness
words fall down
into me
without echo

bound
I still shuffled along
immobile
I kept returning
and started over

5

I said I am an animal
you said you are my animal
I said I am darkness
you said you are of my essence

I said I didn't know you
but spoke in you
fled from you
carried by you

I said I am a shade
you said you are my shade

I can wait and I can go
I can kill you
for you are within me

I fled not knowing
I pursued behind you
it's good you are not
and never will be

I want to turn around
speak to friends
I want once more to bind myself
with the strengthless knots

oh how easily
your hands let me go

o my light
it's good you're leaving
o good light
it's good you flee
great inhuman
light it's good you are not
and never will be

6

He knew
he could answer

it was the most important question

we spoke of many things
of people and poems
I always had that question
ready hidden
but put it off
thought I still had time
later
I'll ask him
then I'll know

I won't ask anything more

Such questions should not be asked

7

Will we create beauty

will I remember
how to write poems
it's not our fault
that instead of lovely
good and happy creations
we give birth to monsters

it's with you
with your conception
with your terror
screaming and silence
we crossbreed and splice
we create with you

monsters
mouthless without light
faithless honorless

faces smeared with tears and whiskey
scars from the collar
scars from the whip

together we create
those wild misshapen forms
growling and grumbling
howling and blubbering
clicking and silence

8

fearfully with weak hands
he clings to life
a dark clod of dung
warm continually fertile

he seeks the broken threads
with a humble smile
catches his breath
once again he does not know
how to speak

Comes the great light
cruel and cold
cuts him off swallows him
spits him out And dies

DEATH

A wall a window
behind the door
the thin voice of a child

beyond the window a street
a streetcar
in come King Herod
the devil death

I give the king a dime
and kick the whole bunch
out the door

death is
real
he looks back
and shakes his finger at me

PERSUASION

Don't be afraid
this is your room
look here's the table there's the closet
an apple on the table
you're afraid of the furniture
silly
that man won't come any more

You're afraid of a chair
an old newspaper a pen
you're imagining things
you're acting very strangely
you just want to get attention

Smile that man won't come any more
look us in the eyes
don't hide in the corners
don't stand against the wall
after all nobody's ordering you
to stand against the wall

say something

UNKNOWN LETTER

But Jesus bent over
and wrote with his finger
on the earth
and again bent over
and wrote on the earth

Mother they are so ignorant
and naive that I have to show
miracles I do such silly
and unnecessary things
but you understand
and forgive your son
I change water to wine
I revive the dead
I walk on the sea

they are like little children
it's always necessary
to show them something new
can you imagine

When
Matthew Mark Luke and John
approached him
he covered the letters
and erased them
forever

VII
from *TWARZ*
(1964)

LAUGHTER

The cage was closed so long
a bird hatched

the bird was silent so long
the cage opened
rusting in silence

the silence lasted so long
behind the black bars
burst out laughter

eerie
quality

Time passing
hopelessly
without
change
only wasting
away

&
indifference

# # #

Assisi a nest
in a cracked cliff
white birds
egg

I carried
that rosy picture
toward
my city

I didn't make it

On the third day
your smile
began to rot
I gave you
to the earth

the river
of forgetfulness
flows over eyes lips
over your feet
dressed in
paper slippers

TALENT

I sat by the wall
with eyes closed
face turned toward the sun
hands closed in a fist

in idyllic childhood
angelic diabolic childhood
I gave pennies
bits of bread
to beggars
they showed me stumps
split from the trunk
empty sleeves
open maws
scabs

finger by finger you pry open
two empty palms
turn the guts inside out
unwind the eyelids nothing

when my teeth were pried open
under the tongue was found
a black penny
alms from
the sun god

THE DREAM OF JOHN

John fell asleep
on the breast of the Master

he saw himself
with the face of Judas
felt the heft of
the moneybag in his hand
kissed the godly face

he did it all
because he was chosen

the tree was covered
with leaves and flowers
the fruit in secret
ripened
and fell

Awake
he saw that love and hate
are like the left hand
resting
motionless
on the lap

I BUILD

I walk on glass
on a mirror
that breaks

I walk on the skull
of Yorick
I walk on this crumbling
world

and build a house
a castle on the ice
everything in it
is prepared for the siege

only I am surprised
weaponless
outside the walls

MY BODY

My body

is a forty year old
household animal
it makes a racket
opens
gives unclear signs
springtime
and at dusk
inside me whirl
heavy white birds
with round blind
breasts

they scream
and beat their wings

FALLING

Or concerning vertical and horizontal
elements in the life of contemporary man

Of old
long long ago
there were real depths
a man might hit

a man who found himself in the depths
thanks to his own foolishness
or the help of his neighbors
was looked at with horror
with interest
with hatred
with joy
he was an example
he lifted himself out
rose up
dripping

Those were solid depths
in fact you could say
they were middle-class

separate depths were reserved for gentlemen
and separate depths for ladies
in the old days

for example fallen women
were compromised
there were bankrupt people
a species almost unknown
to modern law
a politician had his depths
so did a minister a merchant an officer
a clerk a scholar

once upon a time there were also other depths
now they exist only in dim memories
but there are no longer depths
and nobody
can hit bottom
or lie in the depths

The depths our parents
remember
were something fixed
to be in the depths
moreover
was something
definite
a hard case
a lost man
a man who
lifts himself
from the depths

from the depths it was also possible
to throw up your hands to call from the depths
at present those gestures
have no wider meaning
in the contemporary world
depths were removed

continual falling
does not make for picturesque postures
fixed positions

La Chute The Fall
is perhaps still possible
only in literature
in a dream in fever
you remember the tale

about a decent man

who did not come to the aid
of a man committing an "immoral" act
he lied he was slapped in the face
for his confession
the great now-dead maybe the last
modern moralist a Frenchman
received an award
in 1957

how innocent were the falls

you remember
long long ago
The Confessions
of the bishop of Hippo

In the neighborhood of our vineyard was a pear tree, full of
fruit, unalluring either in shape or in taste. We gave ourselves
over to shaking it and gathering the pears, dishonorable
youths, late
at night, keeping up the game on the playground even onto that
hour
because of senseless custom. We gathered therefrom a great
amount,
not for our feast, but, it seems to me, to throw to the swine,
although
some we ate; we gave ourselves over to this pastime the more
because it
was forbidden.
Behold my heart, O God, behold my heart upon which you
took pity when
it was in the depths of the abyss . . .

"the depths of the abyss"

sinners and penitents

holy martyrs of literature
my beloved lambs
you are like children at the breast
who will enter the Kingdom
(a shame there isn't one)

"Does your holiness believe in God?" Stavrogin asked again.
"I believe."
"It is said that faith moves mountains. When you believe and command
a mountain to move, it moves . . . excuse me for mixing up the facts. But
it nevertheless interests me: can your holiness move mountains?"

such questions asked "the monster" Stavrogin
and can you remember his dream
a picture of Claude Lorraine
in the Dresden Gallery
"beautiful people lived here"

Camus
La Chute The Fall

My dear fellow, for the man who is alone,
without god and without a master, the weight of days is terrible

that champion with the heart of a child
imagined
that the concentric canals of Amsterdam
are circles of hell
a middle-class hell
of course
"we are here in the last circle"
he used to say to a chance acquaintance
in a bar
The last
the last moralist

of French literature
carried with him from childhood
his faith in The Depths
He had to believe deeply in Man
he had to love Dostoyevsky deeply
he had to suffer because of the fact
that hell does not exist nor heaven
nor a Lamb
nor lies
he thought he discovered the depths
that he lay in the depths
that he fell

Meanwhile

there were no depths
in spite of herself
a certain girl from Paris
understood that and wrote homework
about copulation Bonjour Tristesse
about death Bonjour Tristesse
and thankful readers
from both sides
of the once so-called
iron curtain
bought her . . .
at any cost
that girl that lady
she's the one
understood that there are no Depths
no circles of hell
no rising up
and no Fall
everything happens
in a known region
not too large
between the
Regio genus anterio

regio pubice
and the regio oralis

and that which once existed
the entrance into hell
was changed
by a fashionable woman writer
into the vestibulum
vaginae

Ask your parents
maybe they still remember
how the old real Depths
looked
the depths of poverty
the depths of life
the moral depths

"Dolce vita"
or Christine Keeler
lived in the depths
the report of Lord Denning
confirmed the complete opposite
Mons pubis
fromt hat height
far and wide spread out
the growing
horizons

where are the heights
where are the chasms
where are the depths

sometimes I have the impression
that the depths depths of contemporaries
lie rather shallow somewhere just under the surface
of life
that is perhaps one more illusion

maybe in our times
there is a need to build
new Depths
adapted to our needs

Mondo Cane
why did that picture
make such a great impression on me
an impression still growing
Mondo Cane ein Faustschlag ins Gesicht
Mondo Cane film without stars
Mondo Cane
there people eat dance kill animals
breed dance pray die
a technicolor report
on the agony of the old
on Chinese cooking
on the agony of a shark
on seasoning
on the burial of old
cars
I remember the crushing of forms
the squeezing of metal
the squeaking and grating
of the annihilated body
the metal intestines of a car
automobile graveyard
one more method of painting
pictures in time with jazz
in Paris the pressing of a body on white canvas
the veil of Saint Veronica
the face of art
the lips of millionaires the lips of their women
fried ants larvae insects
black mounds on silver plates
the lips of the eaters
red lips in Mondo Cane

great shining red lips
move in Mondo Cane

Next a discussion was begun
concerning the third point in the outline
about the church the faithful and the laity
Cardinal Ruffini
said
that the conception of the faithful
is very imprecise
because the third point
did not receive a majority
of votes cast it was sent
to the Liturgical Commission
for further study

In the neighborhood of our vineyard was a pear tree,
full of fruit, unalluring either in shape or in taste . . .
confessed Augustine

did you notice
the insides of modern churches
look like waiting rooms
in a railroad station or airport

Falling we cannot
assume a form
cannot assume
the posture of a heretic
the insignia of power fall
from our hands

falling we tend our gardens
falling we raise children
falling we read the classics
falling we cross out the adjectives

the word *falling* is
not the right word
it does not define the motion
of body and spirit
in which
contemporary man flows

human rebels
fallen angels
fell down headfirst
contemporary man
falls in all directions
at once
down up sideways
in the form of a wind rose

of old one fell
and rose up
vertically
now
one falls
horizontally

VIII

from *WIERSZE I POETMATY*

(1967)

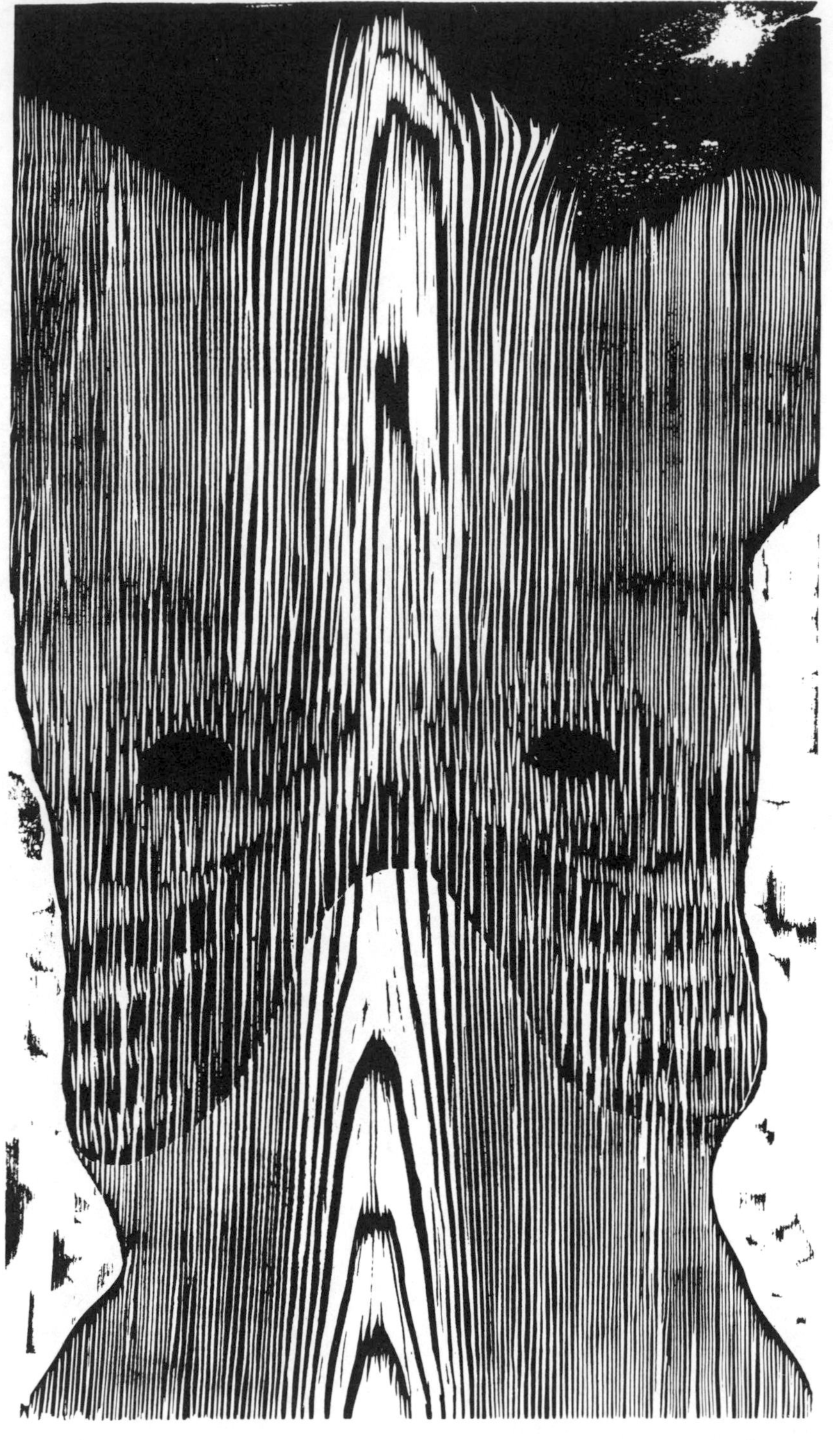

NOTHING IN PROSPERO'S CLOAK

Caliban the slave
taught human speech
waits

with his muzzle in dung
with his feet in paradise
he sniffs man
and waits

nothing arrives
nothing in the magic cloak
of Prospero
nothing from streets and mouths
nothing from pulpits and towers
nothing from loudspeakers
speaks to nothing
about nothing

nothing fertilizes nothing
nothing raises nothing
nothing lives richly
in nothing

nothing waits for nothing
nothing threatens
nothing judges
nothing pardons

IX

from *TWARZ TRZECIA*

(1968)

ACHERON AT TWELVE NOON

A

Enjoying good health
I visited the shores of Acheron

I walked for half an hour or so
in the direction of the railroad station
I passed a bakery
a post office
by an outdoor bar
men stood
drinking beer in slightly-soiled shirts

the snows of yesteryear flowed
newspapers were white
without letters and headlines

do you like street singers
— a stranger suddenly asked me —
I like it very much when someone sings
with a barrel organ
on a cool damp dark
autumn evening

Barrel organ?
autumn evening?
it was some student or other
Lachman Pszoniak maybe Raskolnikov
Dejka Wladek Karbowicz

soon there will be the Ritz theater
and the funeral home
I've walked these streets
for twenty years
milk-white window panes straight letters

wreaths caravans
coffins baby coffins
baby coffins?
probably the joke
of an optimist

walking along these walls
I finished
the forty-fifth year of my life

my heart beat normally
it was twelve o'clock
when I reached
the shore of the canal

in the strings of the rain
on the black mud
white and black butterflies
spread their wings

in the thick black water
nymphs danced
unicorns played
white whales made waves
pink sponges of the lungs breathed
heart
stomach
and womb were visible

in a lower class restaurant
a pimply teen-ager
was biting his fingernails
he crushed flies on the window
crunch

over the dead
festering water
little girls

with green wreaths on their heads
were going to communion

before "departure for America"
Swidrygajłow
drank tepid tea with too much sugar
ate cold veal
looked out of the corner of his eye
at small innocent creatures
and
a slight smile
slowly pulled
at his small
pink lips

from that world
the smell of grits and sausage
came to me
the smell of tripe and bean soup

the snows of yesteryear
flowed

B

I swam
straight ahead swiftly
with lips open
I turned back
terrified by the picture
that waited for me
and grew

with closed lips
I returned to the spring
water was clean alive
I swam the narrowing riverbed

like a throat
inside myself
I was the spring
I wanted
to swim out of myself
return further deeper
earlier

the river was
transparent
shallow shallower
small it disappeared

C

The woods were before us
they will be after us

first by bus
then on horseback
in wagons
one traveled country roads

woods were woods
God God
the Devil the Devil
an apple an apple
a meadow a meadow
a mountain a mountain
truth truth
a tree a tree
lies lies
a horse a horse
night night
parents parents
a river a river

silence silence
death death
life life

in the stove
one lighted pine cones and twigs
at dawn one picked mushrooms
all different kinds
on the stove one cooked
potato pancakes

Jadźka made rye noodles
with milk
the water in the Warta was pure
alive
the mill droned under the white moon
old Marczak
strung fish together

one slept in the barn on hay
or on high pallets stuffed with straw
at night we told each other
the adventures of Jack Texas and Harry Piel
Tom Mix Pat and Patash
Arsen Lupin

Father "dropped in"
after the first of the month
in panama hat and cane
freshly shaved perfumed
bringing newspapers
Mucha Ikac Express
Catholic Guide
mint candy
and waffles
one saved the silver tinfoil
to give to missionaries

to save a little negro
from pagan slavery

the woods were before us

here nobody heard
of Hitler
Uncle Anton remembered
the Russian-Japanese War
in drawers and boxes
roubles lay forgotten
instead of buttons one played
with kopecs
those two-headed eagles

Grandpa ruled the country
the Mother of God
enclosed him in the mantle of her care
villages were smothering
from too many hands unemployed
choking
in rage

In Częstochowa godless communism
and atheism
were condemned
we never saw a communist
gypsies and jews were used to frighten children
Father told the tale
of Macoch and his lover
who played the violin
and had hair down to the ground
Konopacka threw the discus
Kusocinski ran against Nurmi in the Olympics
afterwards we heard
the name Hitler
Grandpa died
the legions of General Franco

fought under the standard
of Christ the king

afterwards it started
afterward it grew by leaps and bounds
on the airwaves
on screens
in the headlines of the newspapers
in thoughts
in our eyes

childhood
sunk down

D

I swam a long time
with closed lips

I turned back

Nobody waited
at the spring at the mouth
nobody
waited on both banks

I go into the depths
I circle
I swim under the surface
here is more life it's warmer
I jump out
my tongue is torn

the hook is no joke
no plaything
hammered out of words

I try to control myself
I want to spit out the bait
but my guts would go with it

then I understand
once again
that my task
is agreement

I recover my ease
lightness
the hair
the rope lengthens
I swim into infinity
together with my time

THE FIRST IS HIDDEN

The first tree

I don't remember
its name
nor the landscape
where it grew

I don't remember
if I came to know
that tree by eye
or ear
if it was rustling
smell or color

if it appeared
in sun
or snow

the first animal

I don't remember
its voice warmth
or shape

all animals
have their names
only the first
is hidden
unknown

DOORS

In a dark room
on a table
stands a glass of red wine

through the open door
I see the landscape of childhood
a kitchen with a blue teakettle
the heart of Jesus in a crown of thorns
the transparent shadow of mother

in the round silence
a rooster crows

the first sin
a white grain in a green
fruit soft
bitter

the first devil
a pink puppet
moving the hemispheres
under a silk polka dot
dress

standing ajar
in the lighted landscape
a third door
and behind it in the fog

far back in the distance
a little to the left
or in the center

I see
nothing

TRANSPARENCIES

I move inside myself
greater
in this dark landscape
a second picture
is hidden
childhood
a white bare field
open very
far away silent
there light appears

two black faces
and a dream

# # #

A couple
old people
step carefully
tenuously

from the foam
naked brilliant whole
without hands or head
the goddess of love
jumps out

a black pit
in the pink
meaty watermelon
of life

the man and women
slowly dip their torn
transparent skins
in the sea

they come out onto the shore
still holding hands

NOTHING

At night
the word *nothing*
grows spreads
violently

in daylight
it loses
its voracity

it slides into life
like a knife in meat

STREAM

Light in the garden arbor
was
yellow agile
frightened as an oriole

the stream
carried in its warm foam
branches
leaves
petals
a white butterfly

I want to hold back
that stream

I throw in a tree
cut from childhood
toys birds faces

I build a dam
that breaks
before my eyes

LINES WRITTEN AT DAWN

I write this poem
in a soft gray color
in silence without light
like in a growing
ball of mold

the paper
under my hand
colorless
limitless rag
dawns

the dead are
transparent
through them I see
great cities a Mouth
a table a book a pitcher
a yellow flower
I hear laughter
they begin to disappear

again they thicken
they overgrow the world

SURRENDER

on all
my towers dreams
on words
on silence
wave white flags

on my hatred
on my love
on poetry
stand white flags

on all
walls landscapes
on the past
and the future
I hung out white flags

on faces
on names
on risings and fallings
wave white flags

from all my windows
flow white flags

in all hands
I hold white flags

CURTAINS

The curtains
in my plays
do not rise
do not fall
do not close
do not open

they rust
rot clatter
fall to pieces

the first is iron
the second rag
the third paper

they fall
piece by piece

on the heads
of the audience
and actors

the curtains
in my plays
sag
over the stage
on the house
in the dressing room

even after the production
closes
they stick to the feet
they rustle
they squeak

X

from *REGIO*

(1969)

REMEMBRANCE FROM A DREAM IN 1963

I dreamed
that Leo Tolstoy

lay in bed
huge as the sun
in his mane
of rumpled fur

a lion

I saw
his head
his face of surging yellow brass
where unbroken light
flowed

suddenly he went out
went dark
and the skin of his hands and face
was rough
broken
like the bark of an oak

I asked him
"what should be done"

"nothing"
he answered

by all his features
his cracks
light flowed toward me

a gigantic radiant smile
burst into flame

HOMEWORK ON THE THEME OF ANGELS

Fallen
angels

are like
little flakes of soot
like abacuses
like cabbage dumplings stuffed
with black rice
they are also like hail
painted red
like blue fire
with a yellow tongue

fallen angels
are like
ants
like moons squeezing behind
the green fingernails of the dead

angels in heaven
are like
the inside of the thighs
of an unripe girl

they are like stars
they shine in shameful places
they are pure as triangles and circles
in their center
silence

fallen angels
are like the open windows of a funeral home
like cow eyes

like bird skeletons
like falling airplanes
like flies on the lungs of fallen soldiers
like strings of autumn rain
joining lips to the flight of birds

a million angels
wander
in the palms of a woman

they are without belly buttons
they write long poems in the form
of a white sail
on sewing machines

you can graft their bodies
onto the trunk of an olive tree

they sleep on the ceiling
they fall drop by drop

# # #

Today I saw Ravenna
in a dream
in the round heaven
white lambs
on a green meadow

golden light flowed
through me

lacrima Christi

# # #

Still in a dream

over a blue sea
sail the ships

rough dry
hair falls
like rust
through my fingers

in fog looms
the outline of day
I run slowly
aground

still in a dream
a white ship sails away
far from the place
where I stand motionless

end to end
black ships red ships
rust

ALPHA

my left hand
illuminates
a manuscript
of the murdered the blinded the burned

song did not escape
whole

my left hand
paints
white as a unicorn
an unreal letter
from the other world

PENETRATION

death
penetrates life
like light
goes through a spider web
hanging on the door
of an open room

the dying man was going
shrieking long seeking
loopholes he came to terms

death ate the features
of successive faces
on the bone

only the hands
cut off earlier
wrote down
the text
and fingerprints
replaced eyes

AKUTAGAVA

Akutagava
in the span of ten years
attained such clarity
in his pictures

that he can be compared
without raising an eyebrow
to a bird
singing
on a leafless tree

in the heart
of a winter landscape

Akutagava
attained such clarity
of language
that he broke
the translation barrier

he was so perfect
and straightforward
that he began to long for death
he put himself to sleep
when he was thirty-six

Akutagava — a Japanese novelist born in 1892 committed suicide

FEEDING TIME

A city appears
out of the smoke and fog
a fat abdomen
covered with neon lights

expires

prostitutes
make mechanical gestures
their faces far away and dead

the voices
of grown-ups rutting
behind a screen
frighten children

tiger god locked
in an iron cage
in the zoo
blinks his yellow eyes

feeding time
has not yet come
the hour of opening

tiger god drowses
among its own
excrement

# # #

white night
dead light
lies on the sheet

white night
ghost of night
on such nights
fruit does not fall
from trees

a poet opened
the veins of poems

in such light
in cold hell
furniture stands
spots on the floor
grow

white night
a dead body
lies on the table
a bloodless animal
on the altar

behind the wall
a man and a woman

blood on the sheets
image of love

###

through a dirty window
in a waiting room
I glanced at

reality

I saw
face to face

weak
I turned away
from my weakness

I turned away
from illusions

on the sand
of my words
someone drew
the sign of the fish
and left

REGIO

Vestibulum Vaginae

in a dark warm
rough
lengthening
cellar

covered
in smothering humidity
potatoes rotted
in spring
milky tusks
sprouted
from their blind eyes

it smelled
of rotting straw
a putrid sweetness

here were celebrated
the secrets
mysteries
of children
the only inhabitants of heaven
on earth

here
nature revealed the secret of sex
revealed the region of the womb
the anus

sweetness swam
dark thick
warm

the cellar
here innocent
as birds dogs
insects
we feverishly sought
the exit
we knew was there
closed
by clenched
lips

rima pudendi

imitating the closely observed
motions of animals
blinded by foreboding
we crawled
from the burrow into the sun

day was catching us
in the clear pupil of its eye
we were returning to light
the vestibule
of the vagina
was closing

Temple

The temple of the god of love
in Kara Korum
stone turtles
in the hourglass of the desert
an eight armed
fat oval
smiling god
his caresses
multiplied one hundred times

so say the enraptured faces
of mortal women

farther on farther on
the same god
but in another form
mounts women
like a horse
the way animals do
he hurls his seed into her

green soft paradise
spreads around
farther hands legs
thighs
on the shoulders
like white wings
raised above the head
where earth was
heaven
in the whites of the eyes
turned upside down
round about
in the oblong
unmoving pupils

transfixed on a phallus
like on a spit
with open mouth
she embraces the god
takes him
in her lips

a mortal

tied up in a faceless knot
bodies
farther on

join
standing
like naked columns

Beyond the black silky water
under the transparent surface
of paradise
the world of the damned
gasps and flames

flying
like leaves
narrow silver
bodies of women
fall into the fire

amid smiling lions
peering tigers
amid bushy fixes and wolves
amid roses and birds of paradise
a phallus forest rises
to the sky

moon and sun roll their radiant heads
around gentle girlish
curves

Vestibulum Vaginae — Return

ripening bodies
hid before
the threatening eye
of bearded god the father

in a dark
warm
lengthening

cellar
sexual organs
joined in imagination
with genitals
of beasts birds insects
with the ovaries of plants

through a little broken window
the light comes in

before our eyes
butterflies joined together in the air
in damp grass toads witches
riotously
mated
a black stallion
mounted
pranced
fell on a mare
a supple phallus
arose from a black sheath
mobile as fire
a whinny filled the sky

it burst the small trembling bodies
a bluish-red flame
danced over the earth

the picture thundered
took flight
our lips were dry
burned
we brushed our thighs against
the tapering backs of galloping animals

gradually
we lost our breath

Mouth Lips

Great heavy white
rounded rising
breasts
of a Sex Bomb
in an open black
fur coat
the lips
large
small lips sweet life

regio
territory land
boundary
a side of heaven
regio femoris
regio orbitalis
regio oralis
the oral region
in the oral region
we distinguish the redness of lips
rubor labiorum

Egg

the world an egg
full
of light

we swarmed
like black spermatazoans
we struck
the impenetrable
membrane

closed it grew
made a rainbow
like a soap bubble
with heaven
turning inside it

it burst under the pressure
of our instincts
it opened
we penetrated
into the landscape
into human meat
into the bodies of animals
colors
tastes
smells
the lips opened
they revealed
a devil
small
as a spark
jumped up to heaven

and stern god the father
in bifocals
said
betrachten wir
unseren Leib
als Tempel Gottes
denn wir nicht entweihen
durfen

the egg of the world
closed
put a thick shell around itself
to wound its enemies

the seed was buried
nakedness hidden
the body grew
more and more sensitive
to pain

the shameful lips
closed

Mons pubis

the night
war drew near

it happened in a nearby
entertainment palace
in a good-time district of a port city

headlines in the newspapers grew
hour by hour
orders were given
the ships of the two superpowers
confronted each other

strip-tease a la Paris
white face
eyes and mouth
carved into it

a woman gave herself
in that hall
to everybody

headlines in newspapers grew
annihilation neared
mechanical music
shrieked

in red light
a tall blonde
stripped
bent over
took off a transparent robe
her thighs shone
in the phosphorescent light
she touched her lips
with her fingers

slowly she opened
her lips
in a cloud of light
she placed her palms
on her womb
ran her hands
along the length of her body

she gave herself to herself
gave herself to objects
to music
to light
falling on her
red blue and gold
she embraced
she hugged
enclosed
an unknown bird
a white swan

rubor laborium

a stream of light
fell on her open face
into her mouth
carrying with it
all the men in the place

she put her hands
on the mound of Venus

when the men
old and young
in white collars
ties
tense yawning
glass in hand
with a smile
they flowed
following the long thin fingers
ending in
ruby silver
nails
when they flowed
to the vestibulum vaginae
a cloud of light
covered the woman
the red of her lips was broken
in the silence fell
the sharp shrieking music

the lights went up
the woman withdrew
in a twinkle opening
her coat
tired smiling
with her face between her legs
she disappeared behind a heavy curtain